The Friendship Dance of Women

Michelle Cullum

DEDICATION

To my husband Earl,
the man whose belief in me
lets me shine.

CONTENTS

INTRODUCTION

1971 was a time when updates on the Vietnam War were broadcast on the evening news. February of 1971 was a time when Apollo 14 landed on the moon and returned to earth. But for me, a little girl of 8½ years, February of 1971 was a time of awaking about other little girls and "friendships."

I was in Mrs. Young's second-grade class with the same classmates I had in first grade and kindergarten. February would bring a special time, a week-long celebration of Valentine's Day. I remember making and decorating my Valentine's-Day sack. Those white paper sacks decorated with pen, glue and glitter sat on the edge of our wood-topped desks for an entire week. Each sack would fill up with "valentines" brought in by classmates every day. The end-of-the-week-Valentine's Day party was something to which we all looked forward. With decorations up, cake and milk served by our moms, games were played; and we didn't have to do any school work that entire afternoon. We were finally allowed to open our 'white sacks' filled with all those wonderful little cards; and some would be extra special because they would also have candy inside. Yes sir, Valentine's Day was a big deal to this 8½ year old little girl.

So why do I remember this Valentine's Day among so many that I celebrated? Unfortunately, I broke out with chicken pox during the week's beginning when we made our sacks; and I was going to miss the 'big party'. Having a younger brother who wasn't showing any signs of chicken pox meant that I was packed off to grandmother's house for the week. Staying with my grandparents took some of the sting out of missing the party. Over the next few days my brother had caught the chicken pox too, so I went back home.

Once back home, my mother showed me the cute animal valentines that she had bought for me to fill out and address to my classmates. She told me how she had gone to school and picked up my missed schoolwork and my Valentine's Day sack. I remember sitting up in my full size bed which seemed huge to me as she put the items next to me. I could hardly wait to open my sack and read my valentines. I had not been forgotten! I was remembered and I felt so special.

With crayons and colored pencils ready to address my classmates' valentines, I was ready to dump my sack and dig in. Everybody was to get a valentine. You didn't leave anyone out; that was just the way it was. You could, of course, make sure to send valentines to the boys that didn't have anything to do with "like" or "love" on them, because frankly, in second grade they were still pretty yucky.

Dumping out my sack and going through it was fun. The selection of valentines in 1971 was limited so of course there were duplicates. On some, the writing was so good you could tell it had been written by a mom. In the middle of my fun I opened a valentine that was from another girl in my class. She was neither friend nor foe, just one of the other girls. The valentine read, "I go ape for you… be my Valentine" with a gray gorilla/ape inside a cage (like at the zoo) on the front. Turning the valentine over I read, "To: Michelle …you look like this" signed From: Sue-Ellen. I don't know how long it took to register what I had read. I know that I flipped it over and thought to myself, "a monkey? I look like that? What? I don't understand. I'm not big like that ape, I don't have gray hair?" Slowly I began to understand that I was being called ugly.

My initial response was to cry. I processed what I read and my feelings were hurt. I felt ugly, friendless, unwanted, not good enough, etc… What happened next was something new to the shy, skinny, glass-wearing 8 ½ year old; I got ANGRY. I sat on my bed and felt anger move through my fingers. I searched through my animal valentines till I found the perfect one. A valentine with a pig on the front and the sentiment, "I go hog wild for You Valentine". Flipping it over in my best hand writing I wrote, "To: Sue-Ellen, you smell like this. From: Michelle" Licking the little white envelope I felt a sense of anxiousness but more than that, I felt strong; and I didn't feel bad at what I was doing. I really was going to do this and I couldn't believe it.

Up until that moment I hadn't really thought too much about that girl. She was smarter than me, dressed cuter than me, was more outgoing than me, and definitely had a lot more friends than me. What had I done to cause her to not like me and think that I was ugly? Well, I would be showing 'her' when she read 'my' valentine. I didn't know it at the time, but the dance between us had started. Over the next several years there would be times when she would lead and when I would lead in both friendship and conflict. Why does this dance start between women? Why do we hurt each other? What makes us continue with this type of behavior? How are we able to turn from conflict to friendship and back to conflict with one another again?

How many of you have a similar version of this story? How many of you can relate to both me and my classmate? There have been times when I have been the giver and receiver of this dance. Perhaps the dance was not easy to spot like reading the valentine. Maybe it was wrapped in an innuendo or told as a joke. Whether the dance is loud and in your face or soft and stealthy, the feelings that arise within each woman are real. This book is written with the hope that women can see the dance we create with other women. You are only able to change what you see and acknowledge.

It is my hope that this book helps you learn the secrets to understanding friendships. This book not only shares with you how to create the friendships you crave but also how to enhance current friendships and yourself. Enjoy the storytelling my friends!.

Michelle Cullum
2011

Michelle Cullum

THE DANCE STARTS

One of the many great perks of living in San Diego is the amazingly great weather. At times during the writing of this book, I would walk over to our community pool to get some sunshine and inspiration. On one such occasion the following scenario between three small girls unfolded right before me.

In the three-foot section of the pool, sitting on the cement steps clinging to a metal handrail, a young little girl shivers in the breeze. From off to the left come two similar aged little girls wearing brightly colored arm floaters. The arm-floaties-girls dog paddle over to the shivering girl.

"Come swim with us" the two implore in harmony. "I can't swim. I've really tried and I don't know why I can't, because I want to but, but I just can't swim" says the shivering girl who now starts crying. "You just need to move your arms and kick your legs like this." The two floaties demonstrate how to kick as they splash water everywhere. The crying, shivering girl now starts to rock back and forth as she says, "I tried, but I can't swim. But I really want too." "Come on," the two say in one last attempt to motivate their friend. "I really can't, I don't know why," the stair-sitting little girl eeks out.

As if there was some unseen queue, the two floater girls look at each other and dog paddle off, giggling and splashing. The little shivering girl, now all alone, continues to hold onto the metal railing watching the other girls have fun.

This whole scenario only took about thirty seconds; and probably twenty-five children and adults were present in the pool. It was one of those moments that happen every day, but I was just so amazed by it.

At such an early age we choose who we want to be with. The two floater girls were having fun, laughing and swimming. Did they realize they had left someone out? Did they see the despair on the other little girl's face? It didn't seem like their actions were done maliciously, but did that matter to the shivering girl who felt left out?

I starting thinking; when and how do we make connections with each other? The dance of friendship starts early. These three little girls could not have been older than three; so when does this dance start?

The first friendship that forms is that between an infant and its mother. Psychologists call this "attachment theory." Research shows that this first attachment has a great impact on how children form friendships, react to unknown situations, and perform in school. A template for future relationships is formed from this early attachment. If infants can and do form attachment relationships with their mother, then when do they start building friendships with others?

While there is no definitive age at which an infant will experience its first friendship, there are three conditions that need to be met in order for friendships to form. The first is that of proximity; infants must be physically near other infants. The second condition is familiarity; infants must consistently be near the same infants. The third condition is mobility; infants must be able to move. When these conditions are met, it is believed that most infants will experience their first friendship with another infant during their first year of life, as early as eight months of age. Interestingly, these friendships are not gender specific. From about eight months old until about four or five years of age, friendships will not be gender specific. Girls will find and have friendships with boys just as easily as they do with other girls. During this time both positive and negative social interactions begin to form. Toddlers engaging with each other, coordinating play with each other, and showing preferences towards their playmates are examples of positive interactions. Negative interactions include disruptions over interpersonal space, competition, and learning to share.

Around the time children are of preschool age, their friendships begin to change and same-gender groups form. Girls now migrate into groups consisting of only girls and boys migrate into groups consisting of only boys. These new same-gender friendships will last until approximately the beginning of adolescence. This separating into girls with girls and boys with boys groups is found throughout many cultures and societies. The now girl-only groups spend more time focusing on relationships and intimacy, while boys-only groups focus on physical activities.

Girls at this age not only group themselves by the same gender, they also begin to exhibit "relational aggression". By the age of three, more girls than boys will show relationally-aggressive tendencies. This 'gender gap' continues to widen as the children age. Relational aggression wounds through real damage to, or threat of damage to friendships, feelings of acceptance, or group inclusion.

How can relational aggression be recognized? These are the predominant characteristics:

- The "silent" treatment
- Rumor spreading
- Non-verbal gesturing
- Body language
- Ganging up on the victim
- "do this or I won't be your friend anymore" ultimatum
- Manipulation

Go back and review the story of the young girls at the pool. Looking at the list of relational aggression, the body language of the two arm-floater girls isolated and separated the non-swimming girl from them. It might be hard to realize and understand, but the impact of relational aggression is just as much, if not more wounding to the victim than is physical aggression.

There are three things that psychologists state every child wants out of life: connection, recognition, and power. Though children desire connection that pulls them into friendships, the want of power and recognition can cause conflict and competition.

The women's dance of friendship is in motion from birth, first with our mothers, and then around age one with everyone else. Around the age of four or five girls become selective with friendships and limit them to only other girls. After the transition into same-gender friendships begins, relational aggression starts to unfold. Within these groups will emerge leaders or "Queen Bees" and followers or "court" of the "Queen Bee". Some girls will be displaced to another group or left to themselves until a new girl comes along.

Several years ago while teaching pre-kindergarten at a local church; I was introduced first hand to the "Queen Bee" and relational-aggression phenomena. My Sunday class consisted of eight girls and two boys who were regular attendees. There was a definite Queen Bee in the group of eight girls. As parents dropped off their children, the girls would group together giggling and waiting for the arrival of **Her.** Each week the arrival of **Her** was welcomed by the girls, each swarming around and vying for **Her** attention first. Week after week I would watch as the girls would show **Her** their new hair ribbon, new shoes, new dress, etc., waiting for **Her** approval. The girls would be met with a statement from **Her**, "That's not new, I have one just like that, mine is prettier," etc., to which the six remaining girls would then immediately gang up with **Her** and start throwing out their own accusations to the one seeking approval. I was always stepping into these small battles doing my best to give approval to the odd girl out and calm the situation. Once things were under control, the focus would then center on who was going to sit by **Her**, who would be **Her** restroom partner, and so it would go for ninety minutes until parent pick-up time.

Something I learned from my Sunday teaching was tenacity about the dance of friendship. Every girl was tenacious, each knowing she would be struck down by standing face to face with the Queen Bee each week, yet still coming back. They would not give up. And you know, after awhile I noticed the reign of **Her** shifted to another girl and then to another and another.

Do you remember a time like this in your life? Psychologists say that most people can remember bits and pieces of their childhood from age four and that by age five memories are stored and can be recalled. Do

you remember this part of your early childhood? What
do you remember about it?

Michelle Cullum

FINDING THE RYTHYM

Can your body really cause you to seek friends and form friendships? The answer may surprise you! Yes indeed! Your body actually responds in a way that helps you seek friends; and form friendships to help de-stress you.

Stress and Friendship

Is there a connection between stress in women, and friendship? And if so, what is that connection? Oxytocin, called the "feel good" hormone, just might be a connection. A landmark UCLA study (ref.1) found that when under stress, women respond differently than do men probably due to interactions between other hormones and oxytocin. A gland in the brain secretes oxytocin into the body resulting in a response that compels women to nurture the young; and to seek out and maintain friendships with other women. This finding suggests that women might have more than just the typical "fight or flight" response that was once thought. When oxytocin is released it acts as a buffer to the "fight or flight" response and encourages gathering with other women and tending to children. By engaging in what researchers termed "tend and befriend", the stress response is countered and in essence, produces a calming effect (ref 2-3). So by spending time with our female friends we are taking advantage of a natural way to deal with stress. This makes sense.

Think about a stressful event that took place this past week. Do you remember it? Ok. Did you pick up your phone and call a friend? How about going to meet them for coffee to talk about it? Now with all the social media outlets e.g., Facebook, Twitter, LinkedIn, and others, it is so easy to reach out to our friends, and there really is no reason not to.

Living Longer

Note: Some of the claims in this section are from a document by Gale Berkowitz that is widely circulating on the world.wide.web, which cannot be completely verified through scientific literature.

The famed Nurses' Health Study from Harvard Medical School found that the more friends women had the less likely they were to develop physical impairments as they aged. The researchers concluded that not having close friends was as bad for your health as smoking or carrying extra weight. Yes you read that correct, not having close friends is as bad for your health as smoking.

Multiple studies have indicated that being in friendships lower the risk of illness due to:

- high blood pressure
- high cholesterol levels
- high heart rates

One study even showed those women who had the most friends over a 9-year time frame cut their risk of death by **more than 60%.**

Bottom line, more friends mean more joy, more calm, and a longer life!

How to Be a BFF (Best Friend Forever)

What are some qualities a best friend possesses? That is what No Nonsense® wanted to find out in their No Nonsense Between Friends Contest. From over 16,000 essays that were submitted, the top 10 tips for being a best friend are:

1. **The Whole Truth and Nothing but the Truth.**
   A real best friend deals in unvarnished truth. Tact is less important than honesty. Be prepared to be on the receiving end as well.

2. **Give What You Take.**
   Best friends recognize they are equals in their responsibilities and need for respect. Have a balanced give and take friendship.

3. **Keeping Secrets.**
   Share your worries with your best friend. Don't hide life-changing events from those who want to be there for you.

4. **Accept Your Friend for Who She is, Not Who You Want Her to Be.**

   Embrace a friend for the gift of who she is. It's okay to be different than your best friend, cherish those unique parts that she brings to the friendship.

5. **Be There.**

   Know when it is best to just listen.

6. **Bask In Her Success.**

   No room in friendship for competitive jealousy. Celebrate her good luck!

7. **Show Up.**

   Be involved in the day-to-day minutiae of each other's lives. Be there for each other in the small events as well as the big events.

8. **Quote Scarlett O'Hara.**

   Friendships, like marriage, have natural cycles of ups and downs and best friends know that, "After all... tomorrow is another day."

9. **Say Thank You.**

   Don't take friendships for granted. Take time to say thanks.

10. Should I Stay or Should I Go.
A best friend is there when you need her and has your best interests at heart. Be honest and know when it's time to cut a toxic friendship loose.

Classic Views
Aristotle gives us great perspective on friendship. He believed that there existed three types of friendships.

1. Friendship based on utility
2. Friendship based on pleasure
3. Perfect friendship based on goodness

Aristotle said,

"Each alike wish good for the other qua good, and they are good in themselves. And it is those who desire the good of their friends for the friend's sake that are most truly friends, because each loves the other for what he is, and not for any incidental quality."

The wish for friendship may develop rapidly, but true friendship does not. It takes time to get to know someone; and to do that you need to share the ups and downs of your lives. What Aristotle says about friendship being based in goodness is a rare quality indeed. The perfect friend should act as a mirror reflecting back love in being just who they are.

Another classic view on friendship comes from Cicero (106-43BC), a Roman statesman who wrote on philosophy.

"Let this, then, be laid down as the first law of friendship, that we should ask from friends, and do for friends, only what is good. But do not let us wait to be asked either: let there be ever an eager readiness, and an absence of hesitation. Let us have the courage to give advice with candor. In friendship, let the influence of friends who give good advice be paramount; and let this influence be used to enforce advice not only in plain-spoken terms, but sometimes, if the case demands it with sharpness; and when so used, let it be obeyed."

Aristotle might have said it first, but perhaps Cicero said it better. Think about doing only good for friends and don't wait to be asked to do it. Does that make you feel a little uncomfortable? How often have you known a friend in circumstances where a home-cooked meal, free babysitting, or fresh flowers could have made them feel like they won the lottery? Have you desired to give advice with candor but failed? "How does this new haircut look?" or "Do I look fat in these?" need I say more.

The belief that close friendships run smoothly and have no problems goes against what these classical men said. All friendships will have conflict at some point. It's necessary to be addressed, and not just swept under the rug as though it never happened. Try thinking "both/and" instead of "either/or" when dealing with conflicts. This type of thinking enables you to remain friends when you do disagree. It's ok to agree to disagree. Learning to live with some discomfort for a short time can kindle your friendship to grow and be healthier and happier.

NEEDING A PARTNER

Connecting

Just how do you find the type of friendships for which you are looking? Think about what qualities you would like in a friend. We all look for similar attributes and connections in friendships. Would you want a friend who appreciated and acknowledged you with these qualities?

- Commitment
- A sense of belonging
- Sees and hears me
- Someone on my side

It is possible to have friendships with women who possess these characteristics. But you will need to seek them out, form the community of friendships you want, and create your own "chosen family".

Choosing

You control into whom to invest your time and energy. Begin by taking an inventory of your current friendships. Determine which are life-giving or life-draining. Ask the following questions about every one of your friends, answering them honestly to identify the "drainers" or "gainers".

1. Can I really be my true self around this friend?
2. Does my friend accept me for who I am?

3. Does my friend help me celebrate my success and listen to me when I have setbacks?
4. Do we both share the same values?
5. Do I feel more energetic and happier after spending time with this friend?
6. Does this friendship offer an equal give-and-take of energy?

What did you learn about your friendships? Did you find there are some friends with whom you would like more community? Are there friends you would like to know better and learn more about? Great! Building relationships with several friends by setting up a simple once-a-month get-together is one great way to grow your "Chosen Family". Maybe your monthly get-together could be club based e.g.: potluck dinner club, desert club, creative expression club, book club, wine club, pampering club, etc.

The possibilities are as endless as your imagination. During your time together learn about each other by sharing information and stories from your lives. Also, a great question resource is found in _If...Questions for the Game of Life_, by Evelyn McFarlane and James Saywell., Villard 1993.

Community
Are you hungry for the types of deep-connecting friendships described in this chapter? You are not alone. In a poll conducted by Dateline, 500 people

were asked how they would spend one extra hour of their time. The overwhelming response from 75% of responders: "with loved ones".

What has created this hunger for more meaningful relationships? Today's adults are so busy with more obligations than ever before, disallowing time for anything else. Usually it is friendships and relationships that first get pushed to the back burner. Even with more technology and gadgets that are designed to help us stay connected with one another, we are further apart. The friendships we do cultivate are only on a superficial level because of our high tech gadgets. Don't get me wrong. We do have connections with others. It's just that they are electronic, not physical. We have the superficial connections of email, texting, Facebook, Twitter, etc... The things that were supposed to make our lives easier are actually just pulling our attention away from each other. They create the need to do and to check on, taking away from our already limited amount of time. The idea of true community is presented, but is it really true community, or just an illusion?

Being busy with obligations isn't the only reason for being disconnected. There are a variety of reasons we miss out on the opportunities to connect with others. Take a look at these statics from Cecile Andrews's book, _The Circle of Simplicity,_ Harper Paperbacks 1998:

- Couples spend an average of 12 minutes a day talking with each other
- The average work week including preparation and commute time is 55 to 80 hours
- Over 50 million people work from home isolated from other people

Between working longer hours and exhaustion, we don't have time for even our spouse let alone friendships. We have to choose to put friendships back on the front burner. I believe authentic friendships make us whole. They heal us and challenge us. Having true friendships not only allows us to learn to love others, we learn to love ourselves. There is no greater gift we can give than that of self love.

Cultivating

Now that you have evaluated your list of current friendships, how do you add to your personal community? Where do you start looking for new friends? This is where you will need to think outside the box! Who have you made regular contact with that you would like to know on a deeper level? Here are some suggestions to get you started: neighbors, colleagues and co-workers, hairdresser, massage therapist, coffee server, etc.

Have you thought about looking in different communities? These are some suggestions of what I mean by community here:

- Spiritual Community
- Professional Community
- Volunteer Community
- School Community
- Friends of Friends
- www.meetup.com
- www.girlfriendcircles.com

Make a list of your possible new friends and then TAKE ACTION. This is the most difficult though important step. Remember, it does not need to be a big step, as long as you are moving forward. That's what counts.

Caring

Once you have searched out and found new friends, you want to invest in and grow these new friendships. Being able to appreciate and acknowledge new friends builds your level of trust and integrity.

Think about the last time someone called you out of the blue or sent you a cute card for no reason. Did this memory bring a smile to your face? I bet it made your day special and gave you joy! If you do this for your friends, you give them an opportunity to experience that same joy. Take a minute to think of three people you can appreciate right now. Think about it and then reach out and touch their lives. They will remember it and they will look forward to your friendship because of your fun and nurturing personality.

Several years ago I worked for a medical staffing company. This was a high stress, high paperwork volume, and never enough time position. I learned firsthand that by nurturing others with the smallest of things could make a huge impact on their day.

Large amounts of paperwork, shuffled between many hands each day, always kept one's "in-box" full. Upon completing my portion of work, I would sign off with my signature and send it on to the next recipient. One day I started adding a smiley face after my signature. The face was nothing fancy, just a circle with two dots for eyes and a curve for a smile. People thought it was cute, laughed a bit, and office life went on.

I left that job in Dallas over seventeen years ago. I received a Christmas card from my old boss of that company a couple of years ago. She wrote in her card, "I always appreciated seeing your smiley face. Regardless of how I was feeling that day, your smiley face always made me smile". What you do does have an effect on others no matter if you think it does or not. Try it for yourself and see what wonderful results you find.

We all have grown up hearing how to treat others, but do we really follow through? In caring for your new friendships go back to the basics and see what a difference it makes to others by adding these four items into your daily routine:

1. Make eye contact
2. Say please
3. Be on time
4. Say thank you

<u>Celebrate</u>

Did you know that September is International Women's Friendship Month? This special celebration was created by Kappa Delta Sorority in 1999 as an opportunity for women to remember their special friends. Their slogan, "Scatter seeds of kindness wherever you go...and watch friendship bloom" incorporates the idea that friends come from a wide variety of places such as over your fence, at the gym, at work or the playground. Friends can be found anywhere.

To learn more about how you can create a special event for you and your friends go to their website, www.womensfriendshipmonth.com.

Michelle Cullum

STEPPING ON TOES

Have you experienced a failed friendship? Chances are you have and so have all the women you know. In fact failed friendships transcend socio-economic status, age, race, and educational background. It happens to all of us but why? Some of the more obvious answers are:

- Moving

- Different Stage of Life (motherhood, marriage, divorce, etc..)

- Not Keeping a Secret

- Returning Borrowed Items Damaged

- Conflict Over a Man

What about those not so obvious answers or when you have no answer at all; like when you are left to figure out what you have done wrong and replay your last meeting over and over in your mind to see if you can find clues as to what happened. You ask your friend what's wrong only to hear, "Nothing, everything is fine." What about those times?

Failed friendship is a topic about which we don't talk yet have all experienced. Women who were once an important part of our lives are now just gone. What happened to all the love and support we gave to each other while friends? All that enriching and respect goes out the window when the friendship is over. Would we accept this type of "avoidance" or non-replies from a dating relationship? I wouldn't! I would be demanding to know what happened, what I did or didn't do, etc... Let's look at how we can be more effective when a friendship ends, whether we or another ends it.

Initiator

There are very few guidelines and no textbooks on "how to break up with a friend". To have some form of closure and dignity for all parties involved, we must talk to one another about how we are going to end our relationships?

Dr. Jan Yager, a friendship expert states, *"For some, admitting to a broken friendship has become like admitting to a failed marriage. Over the last two decades, a myth of a lifelong friendship has emerged, even as the ideal of a lifelong marriage has, sadly, become an unrealistic reality for many people".*

In order to validate one another's feelings and move forward from a failed friendship you need to address the issue, and not just avoid it. What is a good way to do this....write a letter.

Close Your Friendship Letter

- Be as direct as possible
- Convey that you are different kinds of people
- DO NOT blame
- DO NOT accuse

- DO NOT write about past experiences

Writing this type of letter will help the friend you are closing the friendship with to accept the situation without reacting negatively to it. Writing and giving this letter to your intended friend helps you with the closing process and moves you into grieving the loss of this friendship. Some women find that actually picking a date to end a friendship helps with closure.

What would this type of letter look like? Below is a sample letter that shows how to use the points listed:

Dear Sue,

Writing this letter is not easy but needs to be done. My intention with this letter is to close our friendship.

I will always be grateful for the season of friendship that we shared, and will never forget our past times together. Over the time we have known each other our lives have changed and distance has grown between us.

It is time for me to leave this friendship. I acknowledge the need in myself to do this. I didn't want to slowly fade and avoid you; our friendship deserves a proper ending. You deserve an ending without guilt or guessing why it has ended.

I am sorry for any anger or sadness this letter causes you. I wish you nothing but joy, love and peace in your life—always!

Michelle

This type of letter might not be how you want to end a friendship and that's ok. There is really no "right" or "wrong" method to ending a friendship. With a letter at least you can be honest with a friend and let them know you are moving on without leaving them in the dark about why you are avoiding them.

Receiver

What happens when you are the recipient of an ending friendship? Realize that no matter how hard you press your friend on "why" your friendship is ending, you may never know. Some women aren't sure why they choose to end a friendship. If they don't know, they can't explain to you their reasons. Even though it may be hurtful, you will need to move forward and develop new friendships. So how do you know if your friendship is ending? There are some clues to watch for:

- Avoidance

- Unreturned phone calls

- Declined invitations

- Unanswered emails

- Canceling routine dates

When a woman ends a friendship she will have already started to detach herself emotionally before the outward clues begin. By the time she fails to return your calls or avoids you, the emotional aspect is long over. Ending a friendship for the most part doesn't happen overnight, it takes time for the emotional and physical detachment to occur.

If you have noticed some of the clues stated above and are concerned that you have a friendship in trouble, you should confront your friend. You can write her an email or leave a phone message and state the following:

- Your confusion

- Apologize for whatever you may have done that you are unaware of

- Thank her for the great times

This allows you some type of closure over the situation and you are not left wondering and guessing about what is transpiring.

Frenemy

This is a relatively new word, first used in 1977. The Webster Dictionary defines **frenemy**, "one who pretends to be a friend but is actually an enemy." This is the person that walks that line between friend and foe. Who are these people?

- Someone who plays nice to keep tabs on you so that she won't be taken advantage of (especially true in a workplace environment)

- Someone who pretends to be a good friend but betrayal has added a new dynamic.

- Someone who has never really liked you but has decided to keep up appearances. (families are friends, live in same building, run in same social circle)

Frenemies have been around forever. In middle school these were the bullies or "mean girls" that could make you feel like the odd girl out. These people do not have your best interests at heart. If you suspect a friend is really a frenemy, use caution.

I share with you a tale of how frenemies showed up in my adult life. Several years ago I worked in an office of all women. I have to say I was amazed at how a group of women could work together so well and not have "drama" over-run the office. What we could do and accomplish was beyond compare. Each woman brought unique talents that complimented one another. Projects were professional and completed with time to spare. Not only did we work well together we got along well together too. At least that is what I thought.

Many times we went to lunch together. It could be all of us, some of us, or just two of us. So lunch came and off went two and off went three and off went one, me.

Near the end of lunch I heard my cell phone ringing. My boss's name was displayed on the screen so I answered, "Hello". I heard her voice in the background and said again, "Hello" only this time louder thinking we had a bad connection. No luck. A third time I said, "HELLO" but no direct response; however I did hear women talking. I realized I was listening to a conversation that my co-workers had no idea was being listened to.

What to do? What would you do? I would've, could've, should've hung up but I didn't. Being curious, I listened. What I heard over the next several minutes left nothing to the imagination. When I did hang up I realized what a huge dilemma I was in. I now knew the true thoughts and feelings of those who worked alongside me. What do you do with that type of information? I went through the afternoon keeping busy, yet in a haze. I thought a lot about what to do or say. I didn't want to confront them so my only other option was to act like nothing had happened.

That is easier said than done. I became a frenemy to those I worked with who were already frenemies towards me. Wow, does that sentence even make sense. I "played nice" and they "played nice" but deep down it was taking its toll on me. I did eventually leave without ever confronting the women about what I had heard.

I could say the moral of this story is to remember that your cell phone in your pocket, your purse, your bag, or your car can and will redial your last phone number with the slightest nudge so be aware of what and whom you are talking about. The better moral is to confront instead of avoid.

That is what this whole chapter has been about. When a friendship ends we just don't know what to do, so we avoid. Author, Sandy Sheehy while researching her book, _Connecting_ talks about this:

"Friendship lacks sanctions set forth by society to describe its responsibilities. Perhaps that helps explain why the endings are so often irresponsibly and haphazardly executed. Friendship lacks definition in its structure and its bonds. It is described by the experts as one of the very few voluntary relationships that exists, making it more easily prone to rupture."

I hope that you see the importance of confronting when ending a friendship. Whether it is by letter, email, phone-call, or in person it does not matter, just do it. By sharing together we can change what usually is a sad, shameful and silent event, done alone.

DANCING TO YOUR BEAT

I am sure you have heard the expression, "It takes two to tango". In a friendship as in any other relationship it takes two people to make it work. You are one of these two people and in order for you to bring the best to your friendships you have to start with the best you possible. How do you do that? You have to learn how to take care of yourself and put yourself first.

In today's world of wanting everything now and never having enough time for everything it might seem impossible to find the time for friendship let alone time for you. You can find time; you just have to be honest with yourself. What I mean by being honest is to look at everything you are doing. Look at how full your plate really is. Only when you truly see how full your plate is and you realize that you can't add one more "to do" thing on it will you begin to make progress. That's the first step, to acknowledge how full your plate is. The next step is to start clearing off space and make room on your plate for you. When you start doing this you will feel energized and lighter.

You think I'm kidding right. You're sitting there reading this and thinking, "She has no idea how busy I am" or "what does she mean clear off space? She must not have anything to do each day. I can't clear anything off my plate". You're partly right. I don't know exactly what you have on your plate, but I do know that you have a choice about how you live your life. You have a choice on how busy you are. You just need to slow down and evaluate your priorities. Where do you spend your time? How do you spend your time? What and who makes you happy?

Like I said you have a choice. The **big lie** is this, "I don't have a choice."

We all have choices; some choices might be harder than others and might not be easy. In fact some choices might be extremely difficult, but you always have a choice.

Time is finite. That might be something you need to read again, **time is finite**. There are 168 hours in a week. 52 weeks in a year. We all get the same amount of time to use and work with. It is how we use this time that makes a difference. If you have never kept a time log for a week I would highly encourage you to. It can tell a lot about where your time goes and if you are spending your time in the best possible way for you.

Where do friendships fit into your time schedule? We learned from an earlier chapter that friendships are good for health and lead to a longer life. Yet, how often have you put your friendships on the back burner because you didn't have enough time to go around? It's a paradox isn't it! We need friends to be healthier, happier and live longer yet we don't have time for friends so we don't get the benefits of healthier, happier and longer life because we don't have time. Does that make sense to you? It sure didn't make sense to me.

Now that I have your attention, let's see how to find the time for you and for friendships. The first thing to do is to have a great relationship with you, before having a great relationship with others. How do you have a great relationship with you? Simple, you date yourself.

Dating Me

1. Schedule time once a week for a date with myself; thirty to sixty minutes where I can get to know me. I will spend time finding out my likes and dreams, what I want from life and not what others want for me. I will give myself permission to experience the joy of nowhere to be.

2. Journal as much as I can. Purchase a journal just for me. Don't just get a spiral notebook; go find a journal that represents me, that will be special. Take time choosing the right size, color and design. I will remember it is not about how I write, but more about just putting my words on paper and uncluttering my mind. I don't have to fill the page. I can start small by writing

a sentence. My first journal entry will be, *this journal is special because*.......

3. I will work towards sleeping the same number of hours each night, about 8. I will keep my go-to-bed and wake-up time as near identical as possible. If I do stay up or sleep in, I will try to be no more than 1 hour off.

4. I will walk daily. If I walk to the mailbox and back, great. If I walk around the block, great. If I walk for 30 minutes great. I understand that any amount of walking is better than none. Getting outside and moving will get my energy flowing and the endorphins pumping. I will remember that I am the most important part of my life...me. Nobody can change me except me.

5. I am what I eat. Eating breakfast and not skipping meals will help to keep my blood sugar steady throughout the day. I will eat my biggest meals for breakfast and lunch. I will make sure to drink enough fluid for my body. I will take the vitamins and minerals that I need.

Where did these five ideas come from? The journaling and the self-date idea are based on *The Artist Way*, Julia Cameron, Pan Macmillan, 1997.

She states, "Morning Pages are three pages of longhand, stream of consciousness writing, done first thing in the morning. There is no wrong way to do Morning Pages-- they are not high art. They are about anything and everything that crosses your mind-- and they are for your eyes only. The Artist Date is a once-weekly, festive, solo expedition to explore something that interests you. The Artist Date need not be overtly "artistic"-- think mischief more than mastery."

The last three ideas are from *The Self-Esteem Workbook*, Glenn Schiraldi, Ph.D., New Harbinger 2001. He writes, "The mind and body are connected. So often people who feel stressed, fatigued, and mentally "down" are under-exercised, undernourished, and under-rested. You can't ignore your body and expect to feel good."

I always tell my life coaching clients, "You have to put yourself at the top of your To-Do list. Look at it like being on an airplane when they tell you to put the oxygen mask on yourself first then the other person because if you are passed out or dead you are no good to anybody else. Same thing with your life, you are no good to anybody else when you are worn out, frazzled and/or stressed out. Taking care of yourself is the best gift you can give your family, friends and co-workers." It really is amazing how having a balanced life and taking care of yourself flows into all other areas of your life. Try it for a month and see what happens. You won't be disappointed.

Introvert or Extrovert

Do you know your personality trait? Are you an introvert or an extrovert? Knowing your own personality can help you with your friendships. Most people are either an introvert or an extrovert. We can display aspects of both traits though, depending on the situation. But for the most part we usually lean more towards one trait. The largest factor in determining which you are is where you derive your energy. Let's take a look at both and see which one sounds more like you.

EXTROVERT

- Very comfortable in groups
- Love crowds
- Self-confident
- Enthusiastic
- Friendly
- Outgoing
- Center of attention
- Easy to get to know
- Don't like spending time alone
- Get their energy from other people

INTROVERT

- Inward Focus
- Strong sense of self

- Extremely witty
- Process emotions, thoughts and observations internally
- More private and less public
- Think before they act
- Are not swayed by others opinions
- Find small talk easy but tiring
- Passionate
- Get their energy from within

So which sounds more like you? Remember, depending on the situation we can display both traits. The introvert- and an extrovert-brain are wired differently. Your trait is not something that you can control, it is the way you are. The introvert has increased blood flow in the frontal lobes, anterior thalamus, and other areas of the brain that have to do with problem solving and making plans.

I myself am an introvert by design. I have no problem getting up in front of a group of women at a networking event and giving a workshop. I enjoy doing it and have a great time, but when it is over I am drained. I feel like a limp noodle. I recharge myself by reading or journaling. Spending that quiet time with me restores my energy and then I am ready to go again. It would be safe to say that if I were an extrovert, I would be energized by the end of a workshop.

In friendships these traits play out in different ways. For an introvert like me, enjoyment comes from smaller gatherings of friends, meeting 1-on-1 for coffee in a quiet place and having an inner core of three to five friends. An extrovert is more likely to have never met someone who wasn't a friend, loves large gatherings with an 'the more the merrier' attitude, and everyone loves to be around him/her.

If you are an introvert you might feel self-conscious walking into a large gathering of friends who are extroverts. The chaos of a large group with lots of noise and conversations that are more superficial will leave you wanting to go home. If you're an extrovert the opposite would be true for you. Having a one-on-one in depth soul and mind conversation would be boring.

Knowing from where you get your energy will help you choose wisely in friendships. If you get your energy from people, then look for friends everywhere you go. Getting your energy from yourself means keeping the inner core close to you. Think about the friends you currently have. Can you see who might be an extrovert? How about an introvert? Learning what brings energy to you and your friends will help grow your friendships. Want to learn more about your personality? You can take the Myers-Brigg personality test at http://www.humanmetrics.com.

In this chapter you have learned that two parts of a friendship are being a good friend to yourself and choosing a friend wisely. A great meditation to say or write in your journal about this very thing comes from Shasta Nelson, President GirlfriendCircles.com, *"I will protect my friendships by giving in strategic and healthy ways that energize me."*

Michelle Cullum

QUESTIONS & ANSWERS

While writing this book I received many questions from visitors to my website, www.thefriendshipdanceofwomen.com. I compiled a list of those questions based on most frequently asked, addressing the top nine here.

Because you are reading this book, you are most likely looking for more connectedness and belonging in your friendships. As you find answers to your friendship questions, my hope is that you will expand your circle of friends. Don't worry, just be you. Show up. Be present. Above all, enjoy the journey.

"Don't walk behind me; I may not lead. Don't walk in front of me; I may not follow. Just walk beside me and be my friend."
Albert Camus

Q. *Is it possible to have too many friends? Can you get so involved in too many lives that you lose track of each friends needs and then are not the best friend you can be to that person?*

A. Yes. Robin Ian MacDonald Dunbar, a British anthropologist and evolutionary biologist, discovered that at most, people will be part of and interconnected within a group of no more than approximately 150 others at any given time. This is because:

1. It is a cognitive challenge for our brain to keep track of anymore people.
2. It is a time-budget issue; there is simply not enough time to build real relationships.

You can definitely lose track of who is who and who needs what. Quality in a friendship is in direct proportion to the amount of quality time you spend together. The less quality time spent with your friend, the less the quality of the friendship. You and your friend could spend hours together and still not develop a quality relationship.

We have a very predictable ripple pattern to our relationships with these 150 people:

- 5 people are our inner core (most close)
- 15 people are the next level (will do favors for you)

- 50 people are the outer circle (have history with them)
- 80 or so people are the fringe (you know who they are)

Also, remember that internet friendships do not offer you the same quality as in-person friendships. An online relationship can help prevent the decay of a friendship but it can in no way take the place of meeting and sharing quality time with your friend. A touch is worth a thousand words any day.

Q. *Why do friendships with women often turn catty?*

A. In her book, <u>The Hite Report on Women Loving Women,</u> Professor Shere Hite talks about how women have an underlying tension in their friendships that promotes **competition** between one another rather than cooperation. Her belief is that if women could overcome this competition and learn to help each other out we would bring in a new kind of 21st-century power based on helping, not **jealousy**.

Our jealousy shows itself in many ways. "Competitiveness comes in a different guise: an awesomely sophisticated game of one-upmanship. And even when we are not getting one over on other women, we are probably still forgetting to give them the respect they deserve." states Professor Hite. It comes down to this, trust one another and put our friend's needs first, ahead of our own. It's in all our best interest to view each other not as competitors but allies.

Q. *Is it wrong that I rely so heavily on modern technology to maintain my friendships?*

A. There is a saying about everything in moderation. I believe that this also applies here. Remember that the information you are sending by texting or instant messaging is immediately visible to the other person. This is neither good nor bad. However, if I'm having a bad self-image day and my friend texts me saying that she has just finished at the gym and has lost 5 lbs this week, chances are I am not going to be as thrilled about it as perhaps I would be at another time when she could tell me this news face to face. Think about it. Does getting a digital "congratulations" really mean the same as hearing your friend's voice saying this to you? Just make sure to evaluate and moderate your use of the technology...it's about connecting not collecting.

Q. *Why do people suddenly turn on or abandon their friends?*

A. Relationship professionals say abandonment is not uncommon even in the best of friendships. It often occurs when we are in transition or change in our lives. There are three general areas of change that impacts relationships the most:

1. Unspoken expectations. Our friends can't be mind readers. We have to tell them what we want in our friendship and what we don't want.

2. Unexpressed communication. When we are upset or angry with a friend most women stuff it down inside and let it turn bitter. By sharing and communicating with each other we can overcome the issues at hand.

3. Lack of attention. This can happen with the addition of a new man in our life or perhaps going to school, having a baby any number of things. Just remember to include your friends into the new roles you take on.

Life happens and before you know it 3 months have gone by. All 3 areas can impact friendships if we let them. You and your friend need to remember to communicate and tell each other what works best for you in the friendship and mark it on your calendars. By being vigilant and working on your friendship you can make it strong and healthy.

Q. *Is it okay to let go of friendships that seem to have run their course?*

A. I would have to say yes it is ok to let a friendship run its course and end. While researching this book, I came across a study done in London which suggests that you will go through 396 friends in a lifetime, but will have only 33 at any one time. When your life changes due to a new job, move, marriage or having children your friendships may change too. You will tend to gravitate towards those whose situation is more like yours and who can support you in your new role. A new type of friend that has emerged is called the "silent friend" thanks to social networking. This type of friend is one you stay in contact with via messages and emails but who you rarely talk to in person. Friendships that have run their course can easily move into a "silent friend" relationship.

Q. *How do you save a friendship that is in trouble?*

A. When you and your friend are in conflict a paradox is created. You need your friend to listen and support you, but it is your friend with whom you are upset. Now, you don't have anyone to talk to making you more irritated about the whole situation. Round and round the wheel goes.

1. Think about the situation. What is really going on? Why are you fighting?
2. Talk to your friend. Face to face...no texting, emails, or IM's. Tell her how you feel about the situation. Ask how she feels about it. Let her know why you want to heal the friendship.
3. Be calm and open. Share from your heart and don't get defensive. Listen to what your friend has to say, really listen.
4. Give or receive an apology. Only do this if you are really sincere. Anything half-hearted comes across as not caring.
5. Learn from the conflict. Understand the "why" and "how" so not to repeat it.
6. Time. A short passage of time may help your friendship to heal.
7. Remember. Friendships can be healed.

You must be the friend who wants to face the conflict and talk about it using the suggestions above. It's not easy but if you have a friendship full of wonderful memories it is so worth it.

Q. *"What does it take to make a friendship?"*

A. There are 4 parts to a complete friendship.

Consistency + Mutual Care + Sharing + Positive Emotion = FRIEND

Consistency is the biggest reason for women to not develop friendships. I'm busy, your busy, we all are busy and don't have the time to commit to friendships. For a friendship to begin and start to grow you need to meet together at least twice a month for 4 to 6 months according to Dr. Paul Dobransky, a board-certified psychiatrist and columnist for Maximum Fitness magazine.

Mutual Care is about how equal are your friendships. Do you both initiate emails, outings and support each other? Or is the friendship a little unbalanced with more taking than giving? You need mutual care or resentment will move into the friendship.

Sharing is a good thing but how much to share. You don't always have to go deep with your stuff. You can go wide with your stuff. Cover a wide range of information and facts about you. Sharing is not easy so go slow and take baby steps.

Positive Emotion means you feel better after spending time with your friend. You should feel happier and have more energy after being with a friend. You should not feel drained and/or worn out.

You can't skip one of the four or your sum total won't add up to a friend. It comes down to what you want. You can have hundreds of acquaintances, or maybe just 2 to 3 really-connected friends with whom you spend time and grow. It's up to you. Just remember you need all **4 parts** to have a friendship that is going to be authentic and real.

Q. *"How does one handle the loss then put yourself out there again to develop other friendships?"*

A. When a friendship comes to an end for whatever reason, you will experience grief. Grief needs to be worked through by each person at their own pace and their own time. You won't be ready for a new friendship until you have dealt with your grief. Once you have then:

- Always be on the lookout for new friends. You never know where and when you might meet somebody that will be your next friend. Learn to communicate with people you meet.

- Determine what you want and don't want in a friend. If you need to, make a list of the qualities your new friend needs to have. How do you want to be treated? What are some "red flags" that you want to make sure to avoid in a friendship?

- See if you have a hobby or interest. You might consider joining a group or club that fits with it. How about volunteering where you could meet new friends?

- Accept those invitations you get from current friends of your family. Go to events and network with those who have a connection to you through a family member.

- If you meet someone you click with make sure to follow up. It's always nice to meet again for coffee, go ahead and you make the initial request.

The main thing to remember is that a friendship won't happen overnight. It takes time to develop into true friendship, so give it some time to develop.

Q. *"What do you do when a friend becomes too needy?"*

A. When a friend always needs something from you it can become draining on the relationship. If the needs occur time and time again you need to take action. You can't change anyone other than yourself.

- Learn to say "no" to her requests.
- Set up boundaries.
- Tell her you need to take care of you right now.
- Take a step back from your relationship. Put some time between visits.
- If necessary end the friendship.

Don't feel guilty about what you are doing. There are some people whose needs cannot be met regardless of what you do. Look at the other relationships this person has and you will most likely see the same neediness also shows up in them.

ABOUT THE AUTHOR

An authentic living coach and writer since 2008, Michelle Cullum is the owner of **A Renaissance Chick**. She operates in the areas of coaching, writing & uniting.

A long time resident of San Diego, California she is a popular speaker and presenter. A proud military wife and mother of three grown sons, Michelle shares her home with her husband and three cats.